Wid

WITHDRAWN

The Picador Book of

Funeral Poems

EDITED BY

Don Paterson

PICADOR

First published 2012 by Picador
an imprint of Pan Macmillan, a division of Macmillan Publishers Limited
Pan Macmillan, 20 New Wharf Road, London N1 9RR
Basingstoke and Oxford
Associated companies throughout the world
www.panmacmillan.com

ISBN 978-0-330-45687-6

Contents

Parting

Grieving

Longing

Remembrance

Comfort

Acknowledgements

W. H. Auden, 'Funeral Blues', copyright © 1976, 1991, The Estate of W. H. Auden; Kate Clanchy, 'Miscarriage, Midwinter', by permission of Macmillan Publishers Ltd; Billy Collins, 'No Time', from *Nine Horses* by Billy Collins, copyright © Billy Collins 2002, by permission of Macmillan Publishers Ltd and Random House, Inc.; Michael Donaghy, 'Not Knowing the Words' and 'Haunts', by permission of Macmillan Publishers Ltd; Ian Duhig, 'Viaduct Love Suicide', by permission of Macmillan Publishers Ltd; Douglas Dunn, 'France' and 'Anniversaries', from *Elegies* by Douglas Dunn, published by Faber and Faber Ltd; Tess Gallagher, 'Yes', from *Moon Crossing Bridge*. Copyright © 1992 by Tess Gallagher. Reprinted with the permission of The Permissions Company, Inc. on behalf of Graywolf Press, Minneapolis, Minnesota, www.graywolfpress.org; Seamus Heaney, 'Clearances', from *The Haw Lantern* by Seamus Heaney, published by Faber and Faber Ltd; Tony Harrison, 'Timer' and 'Long Distance', from *Selected & Collected Poems* (Penguin 2007); Michael Longley, 'Homecoming', from *Gorse Fires* by Michael Longley, published by Jonathan Cape. Reprinted by permission of The Random House Group Ltd; Hugh MacDiarmid, 'Empty Vessel', from *Complete Poems*, 1993, published by Carcanet Press Limited; Antonio Machado, 'Dream' and 'The Eyes', from *Eyes: A Version of Antonio Machado* by Don Paterson, published by Faber and Faber Ltd; Theodore Roethke, 'She', from *Collected Poems* by Theodore Roethke, published by Faber and Faber Ltd.

Introduction

In our deepest grief we turn instinctively to poetry – to comfort and solace us, or to reflect our grief, give it proper public expression, or help us feel less alone in our experience of it. These poems, drawn from many different ages and cultures, remind us that the experience of parting is a timelessly human one: however lonely the loss of someone close might leave us, our mourning is also something that deeply unites us. These poems of parting and passing, of sorrow, longing and healing, will find a deep echo within those who find themselves dealing with such a loss. Some are uplifting, some are heartbreaking; some are written out of great despair, great love, or from a great bravery; some of the poets here have felt broken by their grief, and others ultimately strengthened by it. But whatever the nature of our grief, it is partly assuaged in its finding a voice – and whether that voice is one of private remembrance or public memorial, *The Picador Book of Funeral Poems* will help you towards it.

Passing

To One Shortly to Die

From all the rest I single out you, having a message for
  you,
You are to die – let others tell you what they please, I
  cannot prevaricate,
I am exact and merciless, but I love you – there is no
  escape for you.

Softly I lay my right hand upon you, you just feel it,
I do not argue, I bend my head close and half envelop it,
I sit quietly by, I remain faithful,
I am more than nurse, more than parent or neighbor,
I absolve you from all except yourself spiritual bodily,
  that is eternal, you yourself will surely escape,
The corpse you will leave will be but excrementitious.

The sun bursts through in unlooked-for directions,
Strong thoughts fill you and confidence, you smile,
You forget you are sick, as I forget you are sick,
You do not see the medicines, you do not mind the
  weeping friends,
I am with you,
I exclude others from you, there is nothing to be
  commiserated,
I do not commiserate, I congratulate you.

WALT WHITMAN

France

A dozen sparrows scuttled on the frost.
We watched them play. We stood at the window,
And, if you saw us, then you saw a ghost
In duplicate. I tied her nightgown's bow.
She watched and recognized the passers-by.
Had they looked up, they'd know that she was ill –
'Please, do not draw the curtains when I die' –
From all the flowers on the windowsill.

'It's such a shame,' she said. 'Too ill, too quick.'
'I would have liked us to have gone away.'
We closed our eyes together, dreaming France,
Its meadows, rivers, woods and *jouissance*.
I counted summers, our love's arithmetic.
'Some other day, my love. Some other day.'

DOUGLAS DUNN

To His Dying Brother,
Master William Herrick

Life of my life, take not so soone thy flight,
But stay the time till we have bade Good-night.
Thou hast both Wind and Tide with thee; Thy way
As soone dispatcht is by the Night, as Day.
Let us not then so rudely henceforth goe
Till we have wept, kist, sigh'd, shook hands, or so.
There's paine in parting; and a kind of hell,
When once true-lovers take their last Fare-well.
What? shall we two our endlesse leaves take here
Without a sad looke, or a solemne teare?
He knowes not Love, that hath not this truth proved,
Love is most loth to leave the thing beloved.
Pay we our Vowes, and goe; yet when we part,
Then, even then, I will bequeath my heart
Into thy loving hands: For Ile keep none
To warme my Breast, when thou my Pulse art gone.
No, here Ile last, and walk (a harmless shade)
About this Urne, wherein thy Dust is laid,
To guard it so, as nothing here shall be
Heavy, to hurt those sacred seeds of thee.

ROBERT HERRICK

Given in Farewell
(To a girl of Yang-Chou)

So deep in love, we seem without passion.
While we keep drinking, nothing shows.

Until the sky brightens
the candles will weep for us.

TU MU
(China, 9th Century)

'Carrying mother on my back'

Carrying mother on my back
just for a laugh –
a few steps; then the tears –
there's nothing of her

ISHAKAWA TAKUBOKU
(Japan, 20th Century)

Triad

These be
Three silent things:
The falling snow . . . the hour
Before the dawn . . . the mouth of one
Just dead.

ADELAIDE CRAPSEY

'Because I could not stop for Death'

Because I could not stop for Death –
He kindly stopped for me –
The Carriage held but just Ourselves –
And Immortality.

We slowly drove – He knew no haste
And I had put away
My labor and my leisure too,
For His Civility

We passed the School, where Children strove
At Recess – in the Ring
We passed the Fields of Gazing Grain –
We passed the Setting Sun –

Or rather – He passed Us –
The Dews drew quivering and chill –
For only Gossamer, my Gown –
My Tippet, only Tulle –

We paused before a House that seemed
A Swelling of the Ground –
The Roof was scarcely visible
The Cornice – in the Ground –

Since then – 'tis Centuries – and yet
Feels shorter than the Day
I first surmised the Horses' Heads
Were toward Eternity.

EMILY DICKINSON

from Clearances

In the last minutes he said more to her
Almost than in all their life together.
'You'll be in New Row on Monday night
And I'll come up for you and you'll be glad
When I walk in the door . . . Isn't that right?'
His head was bent down to her propped-up head.
She could not hear but we were overjoyed.
He called her good and girl. Then she was dead,
The searching for a pulsebeat was abandoned
And we all knew one thing by being there.
The space we stood around had been emptied
Into us to keep, it penetrated
Clearances that suddenly stood open.
High cries were felled and a pure change happened.

SEAMUS HEANEY

Crossing the Bar

Sunset and evening star,
   And one clear call for me!
And may there be no moaning of the bar,
   When I put out to sea,

But such a tide as moving seems asleep,
   Too full for sound and foam,
When that which drew from out the boundless deep
   Turns again home.

Twilight and evening bell,
   And after that the dark!
And may there be no sadness of farewell,
   When I embark;

For tho' from out our bourne of Time and Place
   The flood may bear me far,
I hope to see my Pilot face to face
   When I have crost the bar.

ALFRED, LORD TENNYSON

Good

The old man comes out on the hill
and looks down to recall earlier days
in the valley. He sees the stream shine,
the church stand, hears the litter of
children's voices. A chill in the flesh
tells him that death is not far off
now: it is the shadow under the great boughs
of life. His garden has herbs growing.
The kestrel goes by with fresh prey
in its claws. The wind scatters the scent
of wild beans. The tractor operates
on the earth's body. His grandson is there
ploughing; his young wife fetches him
cakes and tea and a dark smile. It is well.

R. S. THOMAS

To Himself

Now will you rest for good,
My worn heart? Dead is the last lie,
That I thought was forever. Dead.

I feel in us the sweet illusions,
nothing but ash and burnt-out desire.
Rest for good: you have
shaken enough. Nothing is worth
your beating, nor does the earth deserve your
   sighs. Life is sour and dull
and there is nothing else.

The world is clay.
Rest now. Despair
your last; to our kind

Fate gives only death. Now despise
yourself, Nature, the sinister
power that secretly commands our
common ruin,
and the infinite vanity of all things.

GIACOMO LEOPARDI

14

'Infancy is what is eternal'

Infancy is what is eternal;
all the rest, all the rest
is brevity, extreme brevity.

ANTONIO PORCHIA

My Sister's Sleep

She fell asleep on Christmas Eve:
At length the long-ungranted shade
Of weary eyelids overweigh'd
The pain nought else might yet relieve.

Our mother, who had lean'd all day
Over the bed from chime to chime,
Then rais'd herself for the first time,
And as she sat her down, did pray.

Her little work-table was spread
With work to finish. For the glare
Made by her candle, she had care
To work some distance from the bed.

Without, there was a cold moon up,
Of winter radiance sheer and thin;
The hollow halo it was in
Was like an icy crystal cup.

Through the small room, with subtle sound
Of flame, by vents the fireshine drove
And redden'd. In its dim alcove
The mirror shed a clearness round.

I had been sitting up some nights,
And my tired mind felt weak and blank;
Like a sharp strengthening wine it drank
The stillness and the broken lights.

Twelve struck. That sound, by dwindling years
Heard in each hour, crept off; and then
The ruffled silence spread again,
Like water that a pebble stirs.

Our mother rose from where she sat:
Her needles, as she laid them down,
Met lightly, and her silken gown
Settled: no other noise than that.

'Glory unto the Newly Born!'
So, as said angels, she did say;
Because we were in Christmas Day,
Though it would still be long till morn.

Just then in the room over us
There was a pushing back of chairs,
As some who had sat unawares
So late, now heard the hour, and rose.

With anxious softly-stepping haste
Our mother went where Margaret lay,
Fearing the sounds o'erhead – should they
Have broken her long watch'd-for rest!

She stoop'd an instant, calm, and turn'd;
But suddenly turn'd back again;
And all her features seem'd in pain
With woe, and her eyes gaz'd and yearn'd.

For my part, I but hid my face,
And held my breath, and spoke no word:
There was none spoken; but I heard
The silence for a little space.

Our mother bow'd herself and wept:
And both my arms fell, and I said,
'God knows I knew that she was dead.'
And there, all white, my sister slept.

Then kneeling, upon Christmas morn
A little after twelve o'clock
We said, ere the first quarter struck,
'Christ's blessing on the newly born!'

DANTE GABRIEL ROSSETTI

Futility

Move him into the sun –
Gently its touch awoke him once,
At home, whispering of fields half-sown.
Always it woke him, even in France,
Until this morning and this snow.
If anything might rouse him now
The kind old sun will know.

Think how it wakes the seeds
Woke once the clays of a cold star.
Are limbs, so dear-achieved, are sides
Full-nerved, still warm, too hard to stir?
Was it for this the clay grew tall?
– O what made fatuous sunbeams toil
To break earth's sleep at all?

WILFRED OWEN

The Viaduct Love Suicide

'Farewell the world,
Farewell to the night';
Farewell my family,
Forgive me this flight.

I did my husband's
Though with him was gone
The last of the good times
For me and our son.

When I needed bread
Life gave me stones;
That fairy-tale giant
Made bread from my bones.

Hard our communion,
A stone for a host:
My son, you are special,
Different from most,

And most take against
The different as strange;
With names if not stones
They take their revenge.

We're turning to air
That no stone can touch.
'You made my life, son,
I love you so much.'

She stepped from the bridge
Her child in her arms
To join with the earth
No providence harms.

Wind from the wheatfields
Blows through Bridgehill
The last light of evening
Falls on Blackhill

It falls still on Consett
And Leadgate and Delves.
This song is over.
Look after yourselves.

IAN DUHIG

*The first two lines of this poem are from Chikamatsu's
'The Sonezaki Love Suicide'.*

The Death-bed

We watch'd her breathing thro' the night,
   Her breathing soft and low,
As in her breast the wave of life
   Kept heaving to and fro.

So silently we seem'd to speak,
   So slowly moved about,
As we had lent her half our powers
   To eke her living out.

Our very hopes belied our fears,
   Our fears our hopes belied –
We thought her dying when she slept,
   And sleeping when she died.

For when the morn came dim and sad,
   And chill with early showers,
Her quiet eyelids closed – she had
   Another morn than ours.

Thomas Hood

Why Did Baby Die

Why did baby die,
Making Father sigh,
Mother cry?

Flowers, that bloom to die,
Make no reply
Of 'why?'
But bow and die.

CHRISTINA ROSSETTI

The Cold Heaven

Suddenly I saw the cold and rook-delighting Heaven
That seemed as though ice burned and was but the more
    ice,
And thereupon imagination and heart were driven
So wild that every casual thought of that and this
Vanished, and left but memories, that should be out of
    season
With the hot blood of youth, of love crossed long ago;
And I took all the blame out of all sense and reason,
Until I cried and trembled and rocked to and fro,
Riddled with light. Ah! when the ghost begins to quicken,
Confusion of the death-bed over, is it sent
Out naked on the roads, as the books say, and stricken
By the injustice of the skies for punishment?

W. B. YEATS

'Along the field as we came by'

Along the field as we came by
A year ago, my love and I,
The aspen over stile and stone
Was talking to itself alone.
'Oh, who are these that kiss and pass?
A country lover and his lass;
Two lovers looking to be wed;
And time shall put them both to bed,
But she shall lie with earth above,
And he beside another love.'

And sure enough beneath the tree
There walks another love with me,
And overhead the aspen heaves
Its rainy-sounding silver leaves;
And I spell nothing in their stir,
But now perhaps they speak to her,
And plain for her to understand
They talk about a time at hand
When I shall sleep with clover clad,
And she beside another lad.

A. E. HOUSMAN

'A slumber did my spirit seal'

A slumber did my spirit seal;
I had no human fears:
She seemed a thing that could not feel
The touch of earthly years.

No motion has she now, no force;
She neither hears nor sees;
Rolled round in earth's diurnal course,
With rocks, and stones, and trees.

WILLIAM WORDSWORTH

Heaven-Haven
A nun takes the veil

I have desired to go
Where springs not fail,
To fields where flies no sharp and sided hail
And a few lilies blow.

And I have asked to be
Where no storms come,
Where the green swell is in the havens dumb,
And out of the swing of the sea.

GERARD MANLEY HOPKINS

Parting

from Sonnets to Orpheus

Be ahead of all departure; learn to act
as if, like the last winter, it was all over.
For among the winters, one is so exact
that wintering it, your heart will last forever.

Die, die through Eurydice – that you might pass
into the pure accord, praising the more, singing
the more; amongst the waning, be the glass
that shudders in the sound of its own ringing.

Be; and at the same time know the state
of non-being, the boundless inner sky,
that this time you might fully honour it.

Take all of nature, its one vast aggregate –
jubilantly multiply it by
the nothing of yourself, and clear the slate.

RAINER MARIA RILKE

Epitaph on monument erected in 1641 by Lady Catherine Dyer to her husband Sir William Dyer in Colmworth Church, Bedfordshire

My dearest dust, could not thy hasty day
Afford thy drowzy patience leave to stay
One hower longer: so that we might either
sate up, or gone to bedd together?
But since thy finisht labor hath possest
Thy weary limbs with early rest,
Enjoy it sweetly: and thy widdowe bride
Shall soone repose her by thy slumbering side.
Whose business, now, is only to prepare
My nightly dress, and call to prayre:
Mine eyes wax heavy and ye day growes old.
The dew falls thick, my beloved growes cold.
Draw, draw ye closed curtaynes: and make room:
My dear, my dearest dust; I come, I come.

CATHERINE DYER

An Exequy to His Matchless,
Never-to-Be-Forgotten Friend

Accept, then shrine of my dead saint,
Instead of dirges, this complaint;
And for sweet flowers to crown thy hearse,
Receive a strew of weeping verse
From thy grieved friend, whom thou might'st see
Quite melted into tears for thee,

Dear loss! since thy untimely fate
My task hath been to meditate
On thee, on thee; thou art the book,
The library whereon I look,
Though almost blind. For thee, loved clay,
I languish out, not live, the day,
Using no other exercise
But what I practice with mine eyes;
By which wet glasses I find out
How lazily time creeps about
To one that mourns: this, only this,
My exercise and business is.
So I compute the weary hours
With sighs dissolved into showers.

Nor wonder if my time go thus
Backward and most preposterous;
Thou hast benighted me, thy set
This eve of blackness did beget,

Who vast my day, though overcast
Before thou hadst thy noontide passed;
And I remember must in tears,
Thou scarce hadst seen so many years
As day tells hours. By thy clear sun
My love and fortune first did run;
But thou wilt never more appear
Folded within my hemisphere,
Since both thy light and motion
Like a fled star is fallen and gone;
And 'twixt me and my soul's dear wish
An earth now interposed is,
Which such a strange eclipse doth make
As never was read in almanac.

I could allow thee for a time
To darken me and my sad clime;
Were it a month, a year, or ten,
I would thy exile live till then,
And all that space my mirth adjourn,
So thou wouldst promise to return;
And putting off thy ashy shroud,
At length disperse this sorrow's cloud.

But woe is me! the longest date
Too narrow is to calculate
These empty hopes; never shall I
Be so much blest as to descry
A glimpse of thee, till that day come
Which shall the earth to cinders doom,
And a fierce fever must calcine
The body of this world-like thine,

My little world! That fit of fire
Once off, our bodies shall aspire
To our souls' bliss; then we shall rise
And view ourselves with clearer eyes
In that calm region where no night
Can hide us from each other's sight.

Meantime, thou hast her, earth: much good
May my harm do thee. Since it stood
With heaven's will I might not call
Her longer mine, I give thee all
My short-lived right and interest
In her whom living I loved best;
With a most free and bounteous grief
I give thee what I could not keep.
Be kind to her, and prithee look
Thou write into thy doomsday book
Each parcel of this rarity
Which in thy casket shrined doth lie.
See that thou make thy reckoning straight,
And yield her back again by weight;
For thou must audit on thy trust
Each grain and atom of this dust,
As thou wilt answer him that lent,
Not gave thee, my dear monument.

So close the ground, and 'bout her shade
Black curtains draw; my bride is laid.
Sleep on, my love, in thy cold bed,
Never to be disquieted!
My last good-night! Thou wilt not wake
Till I thy fate shall overtake;

Till age, or grief, or sickness must
Marry my body to that dust
It so much loves; and fill the room
My heart keeps empty in thy tomb.
Stay for me there; I will not fail
To meet thee in that hollow vale.
And think not much of my delay;
I am already on the way,
And follow thee with all the speed
Desire can make, or sorrows breed.
Each minute is a short degree,
And every hour a step towards thee.
At night when I betake to rest,
Next morn I rise nearer my west
Of life, almost by eight hours' sail,
Than when sleep breathed his drowsy gale.

Thus from the sun my bottom steers,
And my day's compass downward bears;
Nor labor I to stem the tide
Through which to thee I swiftly glide.

'Tis true, with shame and grief I yield,
Thou like the van first took'st the field,
And gotten hast the victory
In thus adventuring to die
Before me, whose more years might crave
A just precedence in the grave.
But hark! my pulse like a soft drum
Beats my approach, tells thee I come;
And slow howe'er my marches be,
I shall at last sit down by thee.

The thought of this bids me go on,
And wait my dissolution.
With hope and comfort. Dear (forgive
The crime), I am content to live
Divided, with but half a heart,
Till we shall meet, and never part.

HENRY KING

To Delia: On Her Endeavouring
to Conceal Her Grief at Parting

Ah! wherefore should my weeping maid suppress
Those gentle signs of undissembled woe?
When from soft love proceeds the deep distress,
Ah, why forbid the willing tears to flow?

Since for my sake each dear translucent drop
Breaks forth, best witness of thy truth sincere,
My lips should drink the precious mixture up,
And, ere it falls, receive the trembling tear.

Trust me, these symptoms of thy faithful heart,
In absence shall my dearest hope sustain;
Delia! since such thy sorrow that we part,
Such when we meet thy joy shall be again.

Hard is that heart, and unsubdued by love,
That feels no pain, nor ever heaves a sigh;
Such hearts the fiercest passions only prove,
Or freeze in cold insensibility.

Oh! then indulge thy grief, nor fear to tell
The gentle source from whence thy sorrows flow,
Nor think it weakness when we love to feel,
Nor think it weakness what we feel to show.

WILLIAM COWPER

On Leaving His Wife

The thick pine
grows on the rocks
in the sea of Iwami
off the Cape of Kara
as the sea-tangle clings
to the rocky beach.

KAKINONOTO HITOMARO
(Japan, 7th Century)

from *In Memoriam A.H.H.*

VII

Dark house, by which once more I stand
Here in the long unlovely street,
Doors, where my heart was used to beat
So quickly, waiting for a hand,

A hand that can be clasp'd no more –
Behold me, for I cannot sleep,
And like a guilty thing I creep
At earliest morning to the door.

He is not here; but far away
The noise of life begins again,
And ghastly thro' the drizzling rain
On the bald street breaks the blank day.

ALFRED, LORD TENNYSON

'And wilt thou leave me thus?'

And wilt thou leave me thus?
Say nay, say nay, for shame,
To save thee from the blame
Of all my grief and grame;
And wilt thou leave me thus?
Say nay, say nay!

And wilt thou leave me thus,
That hath loved thee so long
In wealth and woe among?
And is thy heart so strong
As for to leave me thus?
Say nay, say nay!

And wilt thou leave me thus,
That hath given thee my heart
Never for to depart,
Nother for pain nor smart;
And wilt thou leave me thus?
Say nay, say nay!

And wilt thou leave me thus
And have no more pity
Of him that loveth thee?
Hélas, thy cruelty!
And wilt thou leave me thus?
Say nay, say nay!

SIR THOMAS WYATT

He Hears the Cry of the Sedge

I wander by the edge
Of this desolate lake
Where wind cries in the sedge;
Until the axle break
That keeps the stars in their round,
And hands hurl in the deep
The banners of East and West,
And the girdle of light is unbound,
Your breast will not lie by the breast
Of your beloved in sleep.

W. B. YEATS

To the Memory of Mr Oldham

Farewell, too little and too lately known,
Whom I began to think and call my own;
For sure our souls were near ally'd; and thine
Cast in the same poetic mould with mine.
One common note on either lyre did strike,
And knaves and fools we both abhorr'd alike:
To the same goal did both our studies drive,
The last set out the soonest did arrive.
Thus Nisus fell upon the slippery place,
While his young friend perform'd and won the race.
O early ripe! to thy abundant store
What could advancing age have added more?
It might (what nature never gives the young)
Have taught the numbers of thy native tongue.
But satire needs not those, and wit will shine
Through the harsh cadence of a rugged line.
A noble error, and but seldom made,
When poets are by too much force betray'd.
Thy generous fruits, though gather'd ere their prime
Still show'd a quickness; and maturing time
But mellows what we write to the dull sweets of rhyme.
Once more, hail and farewell; farewell thou young,
But ah too short, Marcellus of our tongue;
Thy brows with ivy, and with laurels bound;
But fate and gloomy night encompass thee around.

JOHN DRYDEN

On My First Son

Farewell, thou child of my right hand, and joy!
My sin was too much hope of thee, loved boy;
Seven years thou wert lent to me, and I thee pay,
Exacted by thy fate, on the just day.
Oh, could I lose all father now! For why
Will man lament the state he should envy
To have so soon 'scaped world's and flesh's rage,
And, if no other misery, yet age?
Rest in soft peace, and, asked, say here doth lie
Ben Jonson his best piece of poetry:
For whose sake, henceforth, all his vows be such
As what he loves may never like too much.

BEN JONSON

The moon hath left the sky;
Lost is the Pleiads' light;
It is midnight
And time slips by;
But on my couch alone I lie.

SAPPHO
(600 BCE)

Silently I climb the Western Tower,
the moon a hook.
The Wu-t'ung trees in the deep courtyard
are closed by the cool Autumn.

That which scissors cannot sever,
And once unravelled is only knotted up again
Is the grief of parting
With a flavour for the heart all its own.

Li Yu
(China, 10th Century)

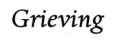

Grieving

from *In Memoriam A.H.H.*

II

Old Yew, which graspest at the stones
That name the under-lying dead,
Thy fibres net the dreamless head,
Thy roots are wrapt about the bones.

The seasons bring the flower again,
And bring the firstling to the flock;
And in the dusk of thee, the clock
Beats out the little lives of men.

O not for thee the glow, the bloom,
Who changest not in any gale,
Nor branding summer suns avail
To touch thy thousand years of gloom:

And gazing on thee, sullen tree,
Sick for thy stubborn hardihood,
I seem to fail from out my blood
And grow incorporate into thee.

ALFRED, LORD TENNYSON

Sorrow

Why does the thin grey strand
Floating up from the forgotten
Cigarette between my fingers,
Why does it trouble me?

Ah, you will understand;
When I carried my mother downstairs,
A few times only, at the beginning
Of her soft-foot malady,

I should find, for a reprimand
To my gaiety, a few long grey hairs
On the breast of my coat; and one by one
I let them float up the dark chimney.

D. H. Lawrence

Grief

I tell you, hopeless grief is passionless;
That only men incredulous of despair,
Half-taught in anguish, through the midnight air
Beat upward to God's throne in loud access
Of shrieking and reproach. Full desertness
In souls as countries lieth silent-bare
Under the blanching, vertical eye-glare
Of the absolute Heavens. Deep-hearted man, express
Grief for thy Dead in silence like to death –
Most like a monumental statue set
In everlasting watch and moveless woe
Till itself crumble to the dust beneath.
Touch it; the marble eyelids are not wet:
If it could weep, it could arise and go.

ELIZABETH BARRETT BROWNING

Funeral Blues

Stop all the clocks, cut off the telephone,
Prevent the dog from barking with a juicy bone,
Silence the pianos and with muffled drum
Bring out the coffin, let the mourners come.

Let aeroplanes circle moaning overhead
Scribbling on the sky the message He Is Dead,
Put crepe bows round the white necks of the public doves,
Let the traffic policemen wear black cotton gloves.

He was my North, my South, my East and West,
My working week and my Sunday rest,
My noon, my midnight, my talk, my song;
I thought that love would last for ever: I was wrong.

The stars are not wanted now: put out every one;
Pack up the moon and dismantle the sun;
Pour away the ocean and sweep up the wood;
For nothing now can ever come to any good.

W. H. AUDEN

Yes

Now we are like that flat cone of sand
in the garden of the Silver Pavilion in Kyoto
designed to appear only in moonlight.

Do you want me to mourn?
Do you want me to wear black?

Or like moonlight on whitest sand
to use your dark, to gleam, to shimmer?

I gleam. I mourn.

TESS GALLAGHER

On the Death of Richard West

In vain to me the smiling Mornings shine,
And reddening Phœbus lifts his golden fire;
The birds in vain their amorous descant join;
Or cheerful fields resume their green attire;
These ears, alas! for other notes repine,
A different object do these eyes require;
My lonely anguish melts no heart but mine;
And in my breast the imperfect joys expire.
Yet Morning smiles the busy race to cheer,
And new-born pleasure brings to happier men;
The fields to all their wonted tribute bear;
To warm their little loves the birds complain;
I fruitless mourn to him that cannot hear,
And weep the more because I weep in vain.

THOMAS GRAY

'Bring, in this timeless grave to throw'

Bring, in this timeless grave to throw,
No cypress, sombre on the snow;
Snap not from the bitter yew
His leaves that live December through;
Break no rosemary, bright with rime
And sparkling to the cruel clime;
Nor plod the winter land to look
For willows in the icy brook
To cast them leafless round him: bring
To spray that ever buds in spring.

But if the Christmas field has kept
Awns the last gleaner overstept,
Or shrivelled flax, whose flower is blue
A single season, never two;
Or if one haulm whose year is o'er
Shivers on the upland frore,
– Oh, bring from hill and stream and plain
Whatever will not flower again,
To give him comfort: he and those
Shall bide eternal bedfellows
Where low upon the couch he lies
Whence he never shall arise.

A. E. HOUSMAN

Empty Vessel

I met ayont the cairney
A lass wi' tousie hair
Singin' till a bairnie
That was nae langer there.

Wunds wi' warlds to swing
Dinna sing sae sweet,
The licht that bends owre a' thing
Is less ta'en up wi't.

HUGH MACDIARMID

No Worst, There Is None

No worst, there is none. Pitched past pitch of grief,
More pangs will, schooled at forepangs, wilder wring.
Comforter, where, where is your comforting?
Mary, mother of us, where is your relief?

My cries heave, herds-long; huddle in a main, a chief-
woe, world-sorrow; on an age-old anvil wince and sing –
Then lull, then leave off. Fury had shrieked 'No ling-
ering! Let me be fell: force I must be brief.'

O the mind, mind has mountains; cliffs of fall
Frightful, sheer, no-man-fathomed. Hold them cheap
May who ne'er hung there. Nor does long our small
Durance deal with that steep or deep. Here! creep,
Wretch, under a comfort serves in a whirlwind: all
Life death does end and each day dies with sleep.

GERARD MANLEY HOPKINS

'I loved her like the leaves'

I loved her like the leaves,
The lush green leaves of spring
That pulled down the willows
on the bank's edge
where we walked
while she was of this world.
I built my life on her.
But man cannot flout
the laws of this world.
To the shimmering wide fields
hidden by the white cloud,
white as white silk scarf
she soared away like the morning bird,
hid from our world like the setting sun.
The child, the gift she left behind –
he cries for food; but always
finding nothing that I might give him,
I pick him up and hold him in my arms.
On the pillows where we lay,
My wife and I, as one,
I pass the daylight lonely till the dusk,
the black night sighing till the dawn.
I grieve and grieve and know no remedy.
I ache and know no road where I might meet her.

KAKINONOTO HITOMARO
(Japan, 7th Century)

'Striving to sing glad songs, I but attain'

Striving to sing glad songs, I but attain
Wild discords sadder than Grief's saddest tune;
As if an owl with his harsh screech should strain
To over-gratulate a thrush of June.
The nightingale upon its thorny spray
Finds inspiration in the sullen dark;
The kindling dawn, the world-wide joyous day
Are inspiration to the soaring lark;
The seas are silent in the sunny calm,
Their anthem surges in the tempest boom;
The skies outroll no solemn thunder psalm
Till they have clothed themselves with clouds of gloom.
My mirth can laugh and talk, but cannot sing;
My grief finds harmonies in everything.

JAMES THOMSON

from *In Memoriam A.H.H.*

I

I held it truth, with him who sings
To one clear harp in divers tones,
That men may rise on stepping-stones
Of their dead selves to higher things.

But who shall so forecast the years
And find in loss a gain to match?
Or reach a hand thro' time to catch
The far-off interest of tears?

Let Love clasp Grief lest both be drown'd,
Let darkness keep her raven gloss:
Ah, sweeter to be drunk with loss,
To dance with death, to beat the ground,

Than that the victor Hours should scorn
The long result of love, and boast,
'Behold the man that loved and lost,
But all he was is overworn.'

ALFRED, LORD TENNYSON

The Poet Laments His Wife's Death

In the evening
they are busy in the reeds,
In the morning
they dive offshore:
but even the wild duck
sleep close by their mates,
lest the hoar-frost
grow on their tails.
They cross their wings
white as the paper-tree
and sweep it away.
As the river's water
does not return,
As the wind's air
Is never seen,
so – being of this earth –
my wife has left
without a trace.
I spread the lonely sleeves
of all the ragged clothes
she made for me
and lie down alone again.

TAJIHI
(Japan, 8th Century)

'Though in great distress'

Though in great distress
at this terrible blow,
I have held onto my life.
But I can't keep my tears.
My tears can't endure my grief.

DOIN HOSHI

from *In Memoriam A.H.H.*

LXXXVIII

Wild bird, whose warble, liquid sweet,
Rings Eden thro' the budded quicks,
O tell me where the senses mix,
O tell me where the passions meet,

Whence radiate: fierce extremes employ
Thy spirits in the darkening leaf,
And in the midmost heart of grief
Thy passion clasps a secret joy:

And I – my harp would prelude woe –
I cannot all command the strings;
The glory of the sum of things
Will flash along the chords and go.

ALFRED, LORD TENNYSON

In Autumn, at a Temple
Near His Wife's Grave

Even at midnight
When I come so rarely –
the wind sad in the pines:
as she lies under the moss
must she listen to it forever?

There is no way out
of this world of ours.
With my heart in torment
I went deep into the mountains,
but even there I heard the stag cry.

FUJIWARA SHUNZEI
(Japan, 12th Century)

Weeping for the Zen Master Po-Yen

Moss covers his bed of stone afresh.
How many springs did my master practice there?
They sketched around him to preserve his form
but burned away the body in the centre.

The pagoda garden closes in the snow.
The library is locked down in its dust.
I hate myself for these streams of tears.
I am not a man who understands the Void.

CHIA TAO
(China, 8th Century)

Bereavement

How stern are the woes of the desolate mourner
As he bends in still grief o'er the hallowed bier,
As enanguished he turns from the laugh of the scorner,
And drops to perfection's remembrance a tear;
When floods of despair down his pale cheeks are streaming,
When no blissful hope on his bosom is beaming,
Or, if lulled for a while, soon he starts from his dreaming,
And finds torn the soft ties to affection so dear.
Ah, when shall day dawn on the night of the grave,
Or summer succeed to the winter of death?
Rest awhile, hapless victim! and Heaven will save
The spirit that hath faded away with the breath.
Eternity points, in its amaranth bower
Where no clouds of fate o'er the sweet prospect lour,
Unspeakable pleasure, of goodness the dower,
When woe fades away like the mist of the heath.

Percy Bysshe Shelley

'She dwelt among the untrodden ways'

She dwelt among the untrodden ways
    Beside the springs of Dove,
A Maid whom there were none to praise
    And very few to love:

A violet by a mossy stone
    Half hidden from the eye!
– Fair as a star, when only one
    is shining in the sky.

She lived unknown, and few could know
    When Lucy ceased to be;
But she is in her grave, and, oh,
    The difference to me!

WILLIAM WORDSWORTH

On His Deceased Wife

Methought I saw my late espoused saint
Brought to me like Alcestis from the grave,
Whom Jove's great son to her glad husband gave,
Rescued from Death by force, though pale and faint.
Mine, as whom washed from spot of child-bed taint
Purification in the old Law did save,
And such as yet once more I trust to have
Full sight of her in heaven without restraint,
Came vested all in white, pure as her mind.
Her face was veiled; yet to my fancied sight
Love, sweetness, goodness, in her person shined
So clear as in no face with more delight.
But O as to embrace me she inclined,
I waked, she fled, and day brought back my night.

JOHN MILTON

Longing

'Even for a moment'

Even for a moment
as short as a joint of the tiny reed
From Naniwa's marsh,
must we never meet again
in this life? Is this what you ask?

ISE
(Japan, 9th Century)

Longing for the Emperor

My Lord has departed
And the time has grown long.
Shall I search in the mountains,
set forth to meet you,
or wait for you here?

No – it would be no life,
to only be longing for you.
Rather I would lie dead
the rock-root as my pillow,

Yet even if it be so
I shall wait for my Lord,
till the dawn's frost
grows on my black hair
trailing fine in the breeze.

In the autumn field,
over the rice-ears,
the morning mist trails,
vanishing, somewhere . . .
My love, can it fade too?

THE EMPRESS IWA NO HIME
(Japan, 3rd Century)

'With rue my heart is laden'

With rue my heart is laden
For golden friends I had,
For many a rose-lipt maiden
And many a lightfoot lad.

By brooks too broad for leaping
The lightfoot boys are laid;
The rose-lipt girls are sleeping
In fields where roses fade.

A. E. HOUSMAN

On the Death of Emperor Tenji

I am of this world
and so unfit to touch a god.
Sundered from his spirit,
In the morning, I grieve my Lord:
if only he were jade
that I might coil on my arm!
if only he were a robe
I might wear forever!

I saw my Lord, my beloved,
Last night; in sleep.

COURT LADY
(Japan, 7th Century)

Miscarriage, Midwinter

For weeks we've been promising
snow. You have in mind
thick flakes and a thick white sky;
you are longing to roll up
a snowman, to give him a hat
and a pebbly smile. We have ice
and I've shown you, under
the lid of the rainwater barrel, a single
spine forming, crystals pricked
to the delicate shape of a fir, but
what can I say to these hard
desolate flakes, dusting our path
like an industrial disaster?
It's dark, but I'm trying to scrape
some together, to mould just
the head of the world's smallest
snowman, but it's too cold and
it powders like ash in my hand.

KATE CLANCHY

A Widow Bird Sate
Mourning for Her Love

A widow bird sate mourning for her Love
Upon a wintry bough;
The frozen wind crept on above,
The freezing stream below.

There was no leaf upon the forest bare,
No flower upon the ground,
And little motion in the air
Except the mill-wheel's sound.

PERCY BYSSHE SHELLEY

'A thousand years, you said'

A thousand years, you said,
As our two hearts melted.
I look at the hand you held
And the ache is too hard to bear.

LADY HEGURI
(Japan, 8th Century)

Fragment 126

My darling

SAPPHO
(600 BCE)

Longing for His Son Furuhi

The seven treasures
that man prizes in this world –
What are they to me?
Furuhi, the white pearl
That was born to us,
With dawn's-star
Would not leave our bed,
but played and romped with us.
With the evening star,
Linking hand with hand,
'Come to bed,' he would say,
'Father, mother, beside me:
I'll sleep in the middle,
Like the triple-stalked sweet daphne.'

Such were his sweet words.
Soon, for good or ill,
We should see him a man –
So we trusted,
As in a great ship.
Then, beyond all thought,
a sudden crosswind
overwhelmed him. Lacking skill
and knowing no cure,
with white hemp I tied my sleeves,
took my mirror in my hand
and, lifting up my eyes to heaven,

prayed to the gods.
My brow I pressed to the ground
Doing reverence to the earth spirits.
'Be he ill or be he well,
It is in your gift, O gods.'
Thus I wailed in my prayer.

Yet no good came of it,
For he wasted away,
Each dawn spoke less,
Until his life ended.
I stood, I leapt, I stamped,
I shrieked, I lay on the ground,
I beat my breast and screamed.
Yet the child I held so tight
Has flown beyond my embrace.
Is this our world's way?

He is too young
To know his way.
Gifts I offer
To the herald of the world below:
O take him on your back.

Offerings I make, and ask,
Do not deceive him:
Conduct him straight,
Teach the way to heaven.

YAMANOUE OKURA
(*Japan, 7th Century*)

Dream

I woke. Was it her breath or my own
that misted up the window of my dream?
My heart's all out of time . . .
The black flame of the cypress in the orchard,
the lemon-blossom in the meadow . . .
then a tear in the clouds,
the land brightening in its lantern
of sun and rain, the sudden rainbow,
then all of it, inverted, minuscule, in each speck
of rain in her black hair!
And I let it slip away again
like a soap-bubble in the wind . . .

ANTONIO MACHADO

'I can take no path'

I can take no path
to meet my love.
Like the high peak
Of Fuji in Suruga –
Shall I burn for ever?

ANON.
(Japan, 8th Century)

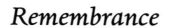

Remembrance

Timer

Gold survives the fire that's hot enough
to make you ashes in a standard urn.
An envelope of coarse official buff
contains your wedding ring which wouldn't burn.

Dad told me I'd to tell them at St James's
that the ring should go in the incinerator.
That 'eternity' inscribed with both their names is
his surety that they'd be together, 'later'.

I signed for the parcelled clothing as the son,
the cardy, apron, pants, bra, dress –

the clerk phoned down: *6–8–8–3–1?*
Has she still her ring on? (Slight pause) Yes!

It's on my warm palm now, your burnished ring!

I feel your ashes, head, arms, breasts, womb, legs,
sift through its circle slowly, like that thing
you used to let me watch to time the eggs.

TONY HARRISON

Music

Music, when soft voices die,
Vibrates in the memory –
Odours, when sweet violets sicken,
Live within the sense they quicken.
Rose leaves, when the rose is dead,
Are heaped for the beloved's bed;
And so thy thoughts, when thou art gone,
Love itself shall slumber on.

PERCY BYSSHE SHELLEY

The Eyes

When his beloved died
he decided to grow old
and shut himself inside
the empty house, alone
with his memories of her
and the big sunny mirror
where she'd fixed her hair.
This great block of gold
he hoarded like a miser,
thinking here, at least,
he'd lock away the past,
keep one thing intact.

But around the first anniversary,
he began to wonder, to his horror,
about her eyes: *Were they brown or black,*
or grey? Green? Christ! 1 can't say . . .

One spring morning, something gave in him;
shouldering his twin grief like a cross,
he shut the front door, turned into the street
and had walked just ten yards, when, from a dark close,
he caught a flash of eyes. He lowered his hat-brim
and walked on . . . *yes, they were like that; like that . . .*

Antonio Machado

To My Father

'It was the First War brought your father down,'
My aunts would say. 'Nobody in our clan
Fell foul of that t.b. Lungs clear and strong
As Trusham church bell, every single one.'

My soldier-father, Devon hill-village boy,
The Doctor's sometime gardener and groom
Hunches before me on a kitchen chair,
Possessed by fearful coughing. Beats the floor

With his ash-stick, curses his lack of luck.
At seven, this was the last I saw of him:
A thin and bony man (as I am now),
Long-faced, large-eyed, struggling to speak to me.

I see him on his allotment, leaning on
A spade to catch his breath. He takes me to
The fair, the Plymouth pantomime, the point
To-point. My mother tells me of how proud

He was when I was five years old and read
The news to him out of his paper. Now,
Seventy years on, he strolls into my dreams:
Immaculate young countryman, his mouth

Twitching with laughter. Always walks ahead
Of me, and I can never catch him up.
I want to take him to the Derby, buy
The wheelbarrow he longed for as a boy.

I want to read out loud to him again.
I speak his name. He never seems to hear.
I know that one day he must stop and turn
His face to me. Wait for me, father. Wait.

CHARLES CAUSLEY

David's Epitaph on Jonathan

Here lyes the fairest Flowre, that stood
In Isr'el's Garden; now, in Blood;
Which, Death to make her Girland gay,
Hath cropt, against her Triumph Day:
Here, here lies Hee, whose Actions pen'd
The perfect Copie of a Frend,
Whose milk-white Vellam did incurre
No least suspition of a Blurre:
Here lyes th'example of a Brother,
Not to bee follow'd by another;
The faire-indented Counter-part
Of David's Joy, of David's Heart:
Rest then; For ever, rest alone;
Thy Ashes can be touch'd by none,
Till Death hath pickt out such another:
Here lyes a Flow'r, a Friend, a Brother.

FRANCIS QUARLES

from *In Memoriam A.H.H.*

C

I climb the hill: from end to end
Of all the landscape underneath,
I find no place that does not breathe
Some gracious memory of my friend;

No gray old grange, or lonely fold,
Or low morass and whispering reed,
Or simple stile from mead to mead,
Or sheepwalk up the windy wold;

Nor hoary knoll of ash and haw
That hears the latest linnet trill,
Nor quarry trench'd along the hill
And haunted by the wrangling daw;

Nor runlet tinkling from the rock;
Nor pastoral rivulet that swerves
To left and right thro' meadowy curves,
That feed the mothers of the flock;

But each has pleased a kindred eye,
And each reflects a kindlier day;
And, leaving these, to pass away,
I think once more he seems to die.

ALFRED, LORD TENNYSON

from Long Distance

(ii)

Though my mother was already two years dead
Dad kept her slippers warming by the gas,
put hot water bottles her side of the bed
and still went to renew her transport pass.

You couldn't just drop in. You had to phone.
He'd put you off an hour to give him time
to clear away her things and look alone
as though his still raw love were such a crime.

He couldn't risk my blight of disbelief
though sure that very soon he'd hear her key
scrape in the rusted lock and end his grief.
He knew she'd just popped out to get the tea.

I believe life ends with death, and that is all.
You haven't both gone shopping; just the same,
in my new black leather phone book there's your name
and the disconnected number I still call.

Tony Harrison

Three Years She Grew in Sun and Shower

Three years she grew in sun and shower;
Then Nature said 'A lovelier flower
On earth was never sown;
This child I to myself will take;
She shall be mine, and I will make
A lady of my own.

'Myself will to my darling be
Both law and impulse: and with me
The girl, in rock and plain,
In earth and heaven, in glade and bower,
Shall feel an overseeing power
To kindle or restrain.

'She shall be sportive as the fawn
That wild with glee across the lawn
Or up the mountain springs;
And her's shall be the breathing balm,
And her's the silence and the calm
Of mute insensate things.

'The floating clouds their state shall lend
To her; for her the willow bend;
Nor shall she fail to see
Even in the motions of the storm
Grace that shall mould the maiden's form
By silent sympathy.

'The stars of midnight shall be dear
To her; and she shall lean her ear
In many a secret place
Where rivulets dance their wayward round,
And beauty born of murmuring sound
Shall pass into her face.

'And vital feelings of delight
Shall rear her form to stately height,
Her virgin bosom swell;
Such thoughts to Lucy I will give
While she and I together live
Here in this happy dell.'

Thus Nature spake – The work was done –
How soon my Lucy's race was run!
She died, and left to me
This heath, this calm and quiet scene;
The memory of what has been,
And never more will be.

WILLIAM WORDSWORTH

To L.H.B. (1894–1915)

Last night for the first time since you were dead
I walked with you, my brother, in a dream.
We were at home again beside the stream
Fringed with tall berry bushes, white and red.
'Don't touch them: they are poisonous,' I said.
But your hand hovered, and I saw a beam
Of strange, bright laughter flying round your head
And as you stooped I saw the berries gleam.
'Don't you remember? We called them Dead Man's Bread!'
I woke and heard the wind moan and the roar
Of the dark water tumbling on the shore.
Where – where is the path of my dream for my eager feet?
By the remembered stream my brother stands
Waiting for me with berries in his hands . . .
'These are my body. Sister, take and eat.'

KATHERINE MANSFIELD

To My Dear Son, Gervase Beaumont

Can I, who have for others oft compiled
The songs of death, forget my sweetest child,
Which, like a flower crushed, with a blast is dead,
And ere full time hangs down his smiling head,
Expecting with clear hope to live anew,
Among the angels fed with heavenly dew?
We have this sign of joy, that many days,
While on the earth his struggling spirit stays,
The name of Jesus in his mouth contains,
His only food, his sleep, his ease from pains.
O may that sound be rooted in my mind,
Of which in him such strong effect I find.
Dear Lord, receive my son, whose winning love
To me was like a friendship, far above
The course of nature, or his tender age;
Whose looks could all my bitter griefs assuage;
Let his pure soul – ordained seven years to be
In that frail body, which was part of me –
Remain my pledge in heaven, as sent to show
How to this port at every step I go.

JOHN BEAUMONT

Epitaph on a Friend

An honest man here lies at rest,
The friend of man, the friend of truth,
The friend of age, and guide of youth:
Few hearts like his, with virtue warm'd,
Few heads with knowledge so inform'd;
If there's another world, he lives in bliss;
If there is none, he made the best of this.

ROBERT BURNS

No Time

In a rush this weekday morning,
I tap the horn as I speed past the cemetery
where my parents are buried
side by side under a smooth slab of granite.

Then, all day long, I think of him rising up
to give me that look
of knowing disapproval
while my mother calmly tells him to lie back down.

BILLY COLLINS

Not Knowing the Words

Before he wearied of the task, he sang a nightly Mass
for the repose of the souls of the faithful departed
and magicked his blood to bourbon and tears
over the ring, the lock of hair, the dry pink dentures.
Was he talking to her? I never learned.
Walk in, he'd pretend to be humming softly,
like wind through a window frame.

The last I saw of him alive, he pressed me to his coat.
It stinks in a sack in my attic like a drowned Alsatian.
It's his silence. Am I talking to him now, as I get it out
and pull its damp night down about my shoulders?
Shall I take up the task, and fill its tweedy skin?
Do I stand here not knowing the words
when someone walks in?

MICHAEL DONAGHY

Epitaph Upon a Child that Died

Here she lies, a pretty bud,
Lately made of flesh and blood:
Who as soon fell fast asleep
As her little eyes did peep.
Give her strewings, but not stir
The earth that lightly covers her.

ROBERT HERRICK

A Quiet Soul

Thy soul within such silent pomp did keep,
As if humanity were lull'd asleep;
So gentle was thy pilgrimage beneath,
Time's unheard feet scarce made less noise,
Of the soft journey which a planet goes:
Life seem'd all calm as its last breath.
A still tranquillity so hush'd thy breast,
As if some Halcyon were its guest,
And there had built her nest;
It hardly now enjoys a greater rest.

JOHN OLDHAM

Song

When I am dead, my dearest,
Sing no sad songs for me;
Plant thou no roses at my head,
Nor shady cypress tree:
Be the green grass above me
With showers and dewdrops wet;
And if thou wilt, remember,
And if thou wilt, forget.

I shall not see the shadow,
I shall not feel the rain;
I shall not hear the nightingale
Sing on, as if in pain;
And dreaming through the twilight
That doth not rise nor set,
Haply I may remember,
And haply may forget.

CHRISTINA ROSSETTI

from When Lilacs Last
in the Dooryard Bloom'd

X

O how shall I warble myself for the dead one there I loved?
And how shall I deck my song for the large sweet soul that
   has gone?
And what shall my perfume be for the grave of him I love?

Sea-winds blown from east and west,
Blown from the Eastern sea and blown from the
Western sea, till there on the prairies meeting,
These and with these and the breath of my chant,
I'll perfume the grave of him I love.

WALT WHITMAN

One Sea-Side Grave

Unmindful of the roses,
Unmindful of the thorn,
A reaper tired reposes
Among his gathered corn:
So might I, till the morn!

Cold as the cold Decembers,
Past as the days that set,
While only one remembers
And all the rest forget, –
But one remembers yet.

CHRISTINA ROSSETTI

Remember

Remember me when I am gone away,
Gone far away into the silent land;
When you can no more hold me by the hand,
Nor I half turn to go, yet turning stay.
Remember me when no more day by day
You tell me of our future that you planned:
Only remember me; you understand
It will be late to counsel then or pray.
Yet if you should forget me for a while
And afterwards remember, do not grieve:
For if the darkness and corruption leave
A vestige of the thoughts that once I had,
Better by far you should forget and smile
Than that you should remember and be sad.

CHRISTINA ROSSETTI

Comfort

Homecoming

The brightest star came out, the day-star, dawn's star
And the seafaring ship drew near to Ithaca, to home
And that harbour named after the old man of the sea, two
Headlands huddling together as breakwater, windbreak,
Haven where complicated vessels float free of moorings
In their actual mooring-places.
                     At the harbour-head
A long-leaved olive overshadows a shadowy cave
Full of bullauns, basins hollowed out of stone, stone
Jars for honey-bees, looms of stone on which are woven
Sea-purplish things – also, inextinguishable springs
And two ways in, one looking north where men descend
While the other faces south, a footpath for the gods.

When they had scrunched ashore at this familiar cove
And disembarked, they lifted Odysseus out of his hollow
Just as he was, linen sheet and glossy rug and all,
And put him to bed on the sand, still lost in sleep.

MICHAEL LONGLEY

'On that faraway mountain'

On that faraway mountain,
Over the ridge, just below the peak –
Look! The cherries are in flower.
May the mists of our closer hills
Not rise up to veil it.

GON-CHUNAGON MASAFUSA

'That it will never come again'

That it will never come again
Is what makes life so sweet.
Believing what we don't believe
Does not exhilarate.

That if it be, it be at best
An ablative estate –
This instigates an appetite
Precisely opposite.

EMILY DICKINSON

Rain on a Grave

Clouds spout upon her
   Their waters amain
   In ruthless disdain, –
Her who but lately
   Had shivered with pain
As at touch of dishonour
If there had lit on her
So coldly, so straightly
   Such arrows of rain:

One who to shelter
   Her delicate head
Would quicken and quicken
   Each tentative tread
If drops chanced to pelt her
   That summertime spills
   In dust-paven rills
When thunder-clouds thicken
   And birds close their bills.

Would that I lay there
   And she were housed here!
Or better, together
Were folded away there
Exposed to one weather
We both, – who would stray there

When sunny the day there,
   Or evening was clear
   At the prime of the year.

Soon will be growing
   Green blades from her mound,
And daisies be showing
   Like stars on the ground,
Till she form part of them –
Ay – the sweet heart of them,
Loved beyond measure
With a child's pleasure
   All her life's round.

THOMAS HARDY

'Do not stand at my grave and weep'

Do not stand at my grave and weep;
I am not there. I do not sleep.
I am a thousand winds that blow.
I am the diamond glints on snow.

I am the sunlight on ripened grain.
I am the gentle autumn rain.
When you awaken in the morning's hush
I am the swift uplifting rush

Of quiet birds in circled flight.
I am the soft stars that shine at night.
Do not stand at my grave and cry;
I am not there. I did not die.

MARY FRY
(20th Century)

'Twas My One Glory

'Twas my one Glory –
Let it be
Remembered
I was owned of Thee

EMILY DICKINSON

Haunts

Don't be afraid, old son, it's only me,
though not as I've appeared before,
on the battlements of your signature,
or margin of a book you can't throw out,
or darkened shop front where your face
first shocks itself into a mask of mine,
but here, alive, one Christmas long ago
when you were three, upstairs, asleep,
and haunting *me* because I conjured you
the way that child you were would cry out
waking in the dark, and when you spoke
in no child's voice but out of radio silence,
the hall clock ticking like a radar blip,
a bottle breaking faintly streets away,
you said, as I say now, *Don't be afraid*.

December 27 1999

MICHAEL DONAGHY

from *In Memoriam A.H.H.*

CXXXI

O living will that shalt endure
When all that seems shall suffer shock,
Rise in the spiritual rock,
Flow thro' our deeds and make them pure,

That we may lift from out of dust
A voice as unto him that hears,
A cry above the conquer'd years
To one that with us works, and trust,

With faith that comes of self-control,
The truths that never can be proved
Until we close with all we loved,
And all we flow from, soul in soul.

ALFRED, LORD TENNYSON

The Widower

For a season there must be pain –
For a little, little space
I shall lose the sight of her face,
Take back the old life again
While She is at rest in her place.
For a season this pain must endure,
For a little, little while
I shall sigh more often than smile
Till Time shall work me a cure,
And the pitiful days beguile.
For that season we must be apart,
For a little length of years,
Till my life's last hour nears,
And, above the beat of my heart,
I hear Her voice in my ears.
But I shall not understand –
Being set on some later love,
Shall not know her for whom I strove,
Till she reach me forth her hand,
Saying, 'Who but I have the right?'
And out of a troubled night
Shall draw me safe to the land.

RUDYARD KIPLING

'Requiem'

Under the wide and starry sky,
Dig the grave and let me lie.
Glad did I live and gladly die,
And I laid me down with a will.

This be the verse you grave for me:
Here he lies where he longed to be;
Home is the sailor, home from sea,
And the hunter home from the hill.

ROBERT LOUIS STEVENSON

'Why hold on to just one life'

Why hold on to just one life
till it is filthy and threadbare?
The sun dies eternally
and wastes a thousand lives each instant.
God has decreed a life for you
and He will give another,
then another and another.

RUMI
(Persia, 13th Century)

Anniversaries

Day by nomadic day
Our anniversaries go by,
Dates anchored in an inner sky,
To utmost ground, interior clay.
   It was September blue
When I walked with you first, my love,
In Roukenglen and Kelvingrove,
Inchinnan's beech-wood avenue.
   That day will still exist
Long after I have joined you where
Rings radiate the dusty air
And bangles bind each powdered wrist.
   Here comes that day again.
What shall I do? Instruct me, dear,
Longanimous encourager,
Sweet Soul in the athletic rain
   And wife now to the weather.

DOUGLAS DUNN

Holy Sonnet X: Death Be Not Proud

Death, be not proud, though some have callèd thee
Mighty and dreadful, for thou art not soe;
For those whom thou think'st thou dost overthrow
Die not, poore death, nor yet canst thou kill me.
From rest and sleep, which yet thy pictures be,
Much pleasure, then from thee much more must flow
And soonest our best men with thee do go,
Rest of their bones and soul's delivery.
Thou art slave to fate, chance, kings and desperate men,
And dost with poison, war and sickness dwell,
And poppy or charms can make us sleep as well,
And better than thy stroke; why swell'st thou then?
One short sleep past, we wake eternally,
And death shall be no more; death, thou shalt die.

JOHN DONNE

'They are all gone into the world of light'

They are all gone into the world of light!
    And I alone sit ling'ring here;
Their very memory is fair and bright,
    And my sad thoughts doth clear.

It glows and glitters in my cloudy breast,
    Like stars upon some gloomy grove,
Or those faint beams in which this hill is dress'd,
    After the sun's remove.

I see them walking in an air of glory,
    Whose light doth trample on my days:
My days, which are at best but dull and hoary,
    Mere glimmering and decays.

O holy Hope! and high Humility,
    High as the heavens above!
These are your walks, and you have show'd them me,
    To kindle my cold love.

Dear, beauteous Death! the jewel of the just,
    Shining nowhere, but in the dark;
What mysteries do lie beyond thy dust,
    Could man outlook that mark!

He that hath found some fledg'd bird's nest, may know
    At first sight, if the bird be flown;
But what fair well or grove he sings in now,
    That is to him unknown.

And yet, as angels in some brighter dreams
    Call to the soul when man doth sleep,
So some strange thoughts transcend our wonted themes,
    And into glory peep.

If a star were confin'd into a tomb,
    Her captive flames must needs burn there;
But when the hand that lock'd her up, gives room,
    She'll shine through all the sphere.

O Father of eternal life, and all
    Created glories under Thee!
Resume Thy spirit from this world of thrall
    Into true liberty.

Either disperse these mists, which blot and fill
    My perspective still as they pass:
Or else remove me hence unto that hill
    Where I shall need no glass.

HENRY VAUGHAN

Epitaph

Rose, O pure contradiction,
Desire,
Nobody's sleep
under so many lids

R.M.R.
December 1875 – 29 December 1916

RAINER MARIA RILKE

She

I think the dead are tender. Shall we kiss? –
My lady laughs, delighting in what is.
If she but sighs, a bird puts out its tongue.
She makes space lonely with a lovely song.
She lilts a low soft language, and I hear
Down long sea-chambers of the inner ear.

We sing together; we sing mouth to mouth.
The garden is a river flowing south.
She cries out loud the soul's own secret joy;
She dances, and the ground bears her away.
She knows the speech of light, and makes it plain
A lively thing can come to life again.

I feel her presence in the common day,
In that slow dark that widens every eye.
She moves as water moves, and comes to me,
Stayed by what was, and pulled by what would he.

THEODORE ROETHKE

Consolation

All are not taken; there are left behind
Living Beloveds, tender looks to bring
And make the daylight still a happy thing,
And tender voices, to make soft the wind:
But if it were not so – if I could find
No love in all this world for comforting,
Nor any path but hollowly did ring
Where 'dust to dust' the love from life disjoin'd;
And if, before those sepulchres unmoving
I stood alone (as some forsaken lamb
Goes bleating up the moors in weary dearth)
Crying 'Where are ye, O my loved and loving?' –
I know a voice would sound, 'Daughter, I AM.
Can I suffice for Heaven and not for earth?'

ELIZABETH BARRETT BROWNING

Index of Authors and Translators

Index of Titles and First Lines